FORESTS

FORESTS

FROM THE AMAZON RAINFOREST TO THE SIBERIAN TAIGA

KIERON CONNOLLY

amber
BOOKS

Published by Amber Books Ltd
United House
North Road
London N7 9DP
United Kingdom
www.amberbooks.co.uk
Instagram: amberbooksltd
Facebook: amberbooks
Twitter: @amberbooks
Pinterest: amberbooksltd

ISBN: 978-1-83886-167-4

Project Editor: Michael Spilling
Designer: Keren Harragan
Picture Research: Terry Forshaw

Printed in China

Contents

Introduction

Coniferous or broadleaf, tropical or temperate, old growth or new – there are many kinds of forests. But then there are three trillion trees on the planet. Without trees, the Earth would be arid and very hot. But by creating canopies, absorbing carbon dioxide and transpiring water back into the atmosphere, trees cool the air and allow other species to live. As environmental author Fred Pearce writes: 'Trees don't just dominate our living world, they made it.'

We may like to think of forests as untouched, but people have been living in the woods for thousands of years. We have hunted there, logged trees for firewood or for timber. We have cleared land for pastures or to grow crops. The sacred groves in different cultures around the world tell us that we find forests spiritual places, too.

We rightly mourn the loss of forests, but, despite immense deforestation, fires and climate change, there are positive cases, from Africa to the Americas to Europe, where trees are reclaiming their space on the planet.

ABOVE:
Douglas firs, MacMillan Provincial Park, British Columbia, Canada
Douglas firs often live for 500 years and sometimes 1,000 years, outliving entire civilisations.

OPPOSITE:
Green Mountain, Ascension Island, South Atlantic
In the 1840s, Ascension Island was arid. Today it has a tropical cloud forest, with bamboo, pine, eucalyptus and banana trees. This was the effort of botanist and explorer Joseph Hooker, who imported trees from around the world. Taking root, the trees enriched the soil and captured rainfall. Once dismissed as a 'cinder', Ascension Island has become a garden.

Europe

The Normans introduced the word 'forest' to England when they invaded in 1066. 'Forest' didn't mean woodland, but uncultivated land set aside for hunting. Many of Europe's forests featured here were first reserved as royal hunting land, but today are open for everybody.

Other forests in these pages are closed for the public's protection. After World War I, the farmland area around Verdun was contaminated with unexploded ordnance. Largely fenced off for a century, what was once farmland is now forest. The conflict can still be seen, not only in the contours of trenches, but the patches of American blue-eyed grass, the seeds of which, it is believed, were imported on the hooves of US Army horses a century ago.

Warfare also makes demands on forests. More than 5,000 English oak trees were used to build HMS *Victory*, Horatio Nelson's ship at the Battle of Trafalgar in 1805. Following the battle, so-called Trafalgar Oaks were planted to replenish the stock.

Between 1750 and 1850, 19 million hectares (47 million acres) of woodland in Europe west of Russia was felled. Today we need to visit the swampy woodland of the Białowieza Forest on the Polish-Belarussian border to see what the central European plain would have looked like centuries ago.

But Europe is now a third more wooded than in 1900. Populations shift, agricultural practices change, and even Iceland has doubled its forest cover.

OPPOSITE:
Trillemarka Rollagsfjell, Buskerud, Norway
One of Norway's largest nature reserves, Trillemarka Rollagsfjell is home to the country's last surviving ancient forest. Some 147 sq km (57 sq miles) in area, the forest is dominated by spruce, with some pine and, in places, deciduous trees. Golden eagles, kestrels and gyrfalcons (*Falco rusticolus*) are regularly sighted.

ALL PHOTOGRAPHS:

Ásbyrgi, Iceland

Not known for its woodland, Iceland has more than doubled its forested land since 1950. But this is still small – only two per cent of the land mass – when you consider that up to 40 per cent of the island was wooded when first settled in the late 9th century. In recent years, successful efforts have been made to fence off areas for woodland regeneration and protect them from grazing sheep.

In the glacial canyon at Ásbyrgi, conifers such as Siberian larch (*Larix sibirica*) and the California poplar (*Populus trichocarpa*) are being planted alongside long-established deciduous species, such as birch, willow and rowan (*Sorbus aucuparia*), pictured above.

ALL PHOTOGRAPHS:
Loch Lomond and Trossachs National Park, Scotland
Situated on the eastern fringe of the Loch Lomond and Trossachs National Park, the wood and copper bridge (right) over the Bracklinn Falls was constructed in 2010 after the previous steel footbridge was washed away in a flood.

In his 1817 novel *Rob Roy*, Walter Scott described Loch Ard (opposite) as 'an enchanting sheet of water'. It is one of Scotland's smaller, land-locked lochs, and the many trees around its edge include Sitka spruce (*Picea sitchensis*), the largest of the spruce species.

OPPOSITE AND TOP LEFT:

Mabie, Dumfries and Galloway, Scotland

With Britain's timber reserves dangerously depleted by 1943, Mabie Forest (opposite) was bought by the Forestry Commission as part of a wartime tree-planting programme. Today its woods include conifers such as Douglas firs (*Pseudotsuga menziesii*), giant sequoia (*Sequoiadendron giganteum*), and larch – a deciduous conifer – as well as deciduous hardwoods, such as beech.

From spring to the first frosts, the wood-rotting Sulphur Tuft fungus (*Hypholoma fasciculare*) (left) helps break down the dead wood and regenerate the forest. The fungus can be found in Mabie on deciduous hardwood and conifer tree stumps.

BOTTOM LEFT:

Pine tree stumps, Glencoe, Highlands, Scotland

Britain's Forestry Commission was established in 1919 after the demands of World War I had almost exhausted the country of timber. Early plantings by the commission favoured conifers, such as in the Highlands where the soil might not support broadleaved woodlands. In recent years, this has been balanced better with more deciduous trees and greater species diversity.

ALL PHOTOGRAPHS:

Wicklow Mountains, County Wicklow, Republic of Ireland

The uplands of the Wicklow Mountains consist of blanket bog, heath and grassland, while the valleys feature coniferous and deciduous woodland. Following centuries of clearances, new afforestation programmes – planting where there previously wasn't woodland – began in the 1920s, mainly with coniferous trees.

Sika deer (*Cervus nippon*) (above) were introduced to the Powerscourt Estate in County Wicklow in 1859. Many have now interbred with the red deer that had been reintroduced during the previous century.

Glendalough (right) is a glacial valley surrounded by semi-natural oak woodland. In around 1042, oak timber from Glendalough was used by the Vikings to build a 30m (94.5ft) longship, the second-longest ever recorded.

Gougane Barra, County Cork, Republic of Ireland
The trees and the moss growing on them might suggest that this is an old forest, but in fact it was only started in 1938. Nestling in a valley on the edge of the Sheehy Mountains, Gougane Barra has Sitka spruce (*Picea sitchensis*) (pictured) and Japanese larch (*Larix kaempferi*), along with pine.

LEFT:

Tollymore, County Down, Northern Ireland
The most common tree species at Tollymore are ash (*Fraxinus excelsior*), beech (*Fagus sylvatica*), birch and oak. During the 19th century, there were a number of water-powered sawmills in the forest. The mills have gone, but the millponds remain. Wood from Tollymore was used in the interiors of RMS *Titanic*, built 56km (35 miles) away in Belfast.

ABOVE:

Cwm Rheidol, Ceredigion, Wales
The ancient-wooded valley of Cwm Rheidol was once dominated by oak and birch trees, but now includes planted pines, larch, spruce and beech. Built in 1902 to carry lead from mines in the valley down to the port of Aberystwyth, the narrow-gauge Vale of Rheidol Railway is today a tourist route.

Forest of Dean, Gloucestershire, England

Although it is ancient woodland, the Forest of Dean has changed many times over the centuries. The Normans kept the forest as a royal hunting ground stocked with wild boar and deer. In the late 13th century, local miners were granted rights to work there, digging initially for iron ore and later coal. Under the Tudors in the 16th century, the forest also became a source of timber for warships. Coal mining continued into the 19th century, with a network of light railways built through the woods to transport the coal.

Today heavy industry has almost entirely ceased, fallow deer have been reintroduced legally and wild boar illegally. The mixed forest contains predominantly oak, beech and sweet chestnut trees.

Unique to Puzzlewood forest (right) are its scowles – geologically formed pits and hollows that were further expanded by miners.

LEFT:

New Forest, Hampshire-Wiltshire, England

The New Forest is new in the sense that it was proclaimed a royal forest for deer hunting by William the Conqueror in around the year 1079. Known for its heathland and thousands of roaming New Forest ponies – a semi-feral breed indigenous to the area – the forest covers 566 sq km (219 sq miles). The grazing ponies help maintain the open heathland. Just under a quarter of the forest is broadleaved woodland and there are also enclosures of conifers grown for timber.

RIGHT:

Grizedale, Cumbria, England

The largest forest in the Lake District, Grizedale's woodland is largely oak, larch, spruce and pine. Pictured is an aerial assault course, but Grizedale also includes many stone and wood sculptures, which are slowly consumed by the trees, moss and lichen.

ALL PHOTOGRAPHS:
Hallerbos, Flemish Brabant, Belgium
Hallerbos was first mentioned in records as far back as 686 CE, but it was almost obliterated during World War I when occupying German forces felled all the big trees. Replanting began after the war, giving Hallerbos the appearance of a young forest. Bluebells (above) thrive on beech trees' leaf mulch, and can flower and pollinate in the spring before the trees' dense canopy closes off the light.

ABOVE:

Compiègne, Oise, France

Just 60km (37 miles) north of Paris, Compiègne has long
been associated with royalty and hunting. Then, in 1918, the
forest provided the necessary privacy for the signing of the 11
November Armistice, marking the formal end of World War I.
The forest's more populous trees are European oak (*Quercus
robur*), beech (*Fagus sylvatica*) and hornbeam (*Carpinus
betulus*). Deer and wild boar can still be found here.

RIGHT:

Fontainebleau, Seine-et-Marne, France

Also known as the Forêt de Bière ('Forest of Heather'),
Fontainebleau is a mixed deciduous forest known for its rock
formations, some of which resemble animals such as an elephant
or a crocodile. Its connections with French royalty date back to
the 12th century when Louis VII built a hunting lodge there.

OPPOSITE:

Landes, Nouvelle-Aquitaine, France

The largest man-made woodland in western Europe, Landes forest was established in the 18th century as a pine plantation to manage erosion and cleanse the soil in a swampy area on France's southwest coast. Today the forest is largely composed of maritime pine (*Pinus pinaster*), grown for wood and paper products.

LEFT:

Verdun, Meuse, France

More than a century on, the lines of trenches and shell craters still shape the landscape at the World War I battleground of Verdun. After the war, with the soil destroyed and littered with deadly unexploded ordnance, the French government designated 120,000 hectares (300,000 acres) of former arable farmland a forbidden zone and resettled the remaining population. Limited reforestation was begun with pine and Norway spruce – species that can thrive in poor soil. In the 1960s, some of these trees were logged and replaced with European beech, a species common in the area. Today, with much of the area remaining off limits and with dangerous ordnance still in the ground, this part of Verdun has become a forest.

Harz Mountains, Lower Saxony, Saxony-Anhalt and Thuringia, Germany
Running west to east across northern Germany, the Harz Mountains (left) support woodlands that contain beech, oak, silver birch (*Betula pendula*) and sycamore (*Acer pseudoplatanus*) at lower altitudes, giving way to spruce at higher levels. Located in the Lower Saxon part of the Harz, the Söse Dam was completed in 1931.

Steam enthusiasts can be grateful that the former East German State Railway didn't fully modernise the narrow-gauge Harz Railway (right). Today, 1950s steam locomotives still pull trains up beyond the tree line to the station serving Brocken, the highest peak in northern Germany.

Black Forest, Baden-Württemberg, Germany
Originally a mixed forest that included firs and deciduous trees, the Black Forest was almost annihilated during the 19th century by intensive forestry. Logs were rafted down rivers for use in the shipping industry, and for timber. In replanting with mainly spruce trees, the forest has lost a great deal of its diversity.

RIGHT:
Białowieza, Poland-Belarus
Northeastern Europe was once covered in forest just like the Białowieza, which straddles the Polish-Belarussian border. Dense and low-lying, for centuries the forest was crossed only by river routes. Later it was protected for hunting bison and, although nearly hunted to extinction in the early 20th century, these animals can still be seen here today. As a primeval forest – one that has reached great age without significant disturbance – its trees include European hornbeam (*Carpinus betulus*), oak, spruce and pine.

OPPOSITE:
Crooked Forest, West Pomerania, Poland
It is not known why the 400 pine trees in this grove bend in such a curious way. The forest was planted in around 1930 and it has been suggested that the trees were manipulated, perhaps because the wood would later be used in furniture or boatbuilding. But the mystery remains.

LEFT:

Myllykoski rapids, Oulanka National Park, Northern Ostrobothnia and Lapland, Finland

Celebrated for its rapids and biodiversity, Oulanka National Park is situated on the Russian border in a mixed Finnish and Sami area of northeastern Finland. Many huts first built for reindeer herders or loggers are now free to use for hikers. At the feet of the spruce and silver birch trees, the forest floor is covered in dark green moss.

RIGHT:

Soomaa National Park, Viljandi, Estonia

Soomaa means 'land of bogs' in Estonian, but almost half of the Soomaa National Park is forest – peatland forest, spruce bog forest and floodplain forest, among others. Along with birches and pines, black alders (*Alnus glutinosa*), which thrive in wet locations, are also common.

East Siberian Taiga, Russia
A musk deer in the taiga – a type of coniferous forest found in the high northern latitudes. The East Siberian taiga has a subarctic climate and relatively dry winters with little snowfall. The Siberian larch (*Larix sibirica*) dominates these woods, with pines, birches, poplars and willow (pictured right bottom) found further south towards Lake Baikal.

East Sayan, Buryatia, Siberia, Russia
A mountain range in the remote republic of Buryatia in southern Siberia, the Sayan once served as a border between Russia and Mongolia. Its trees include Siberian pines (*Pinus sibirica*) (pictured). The Russian far north contains a quarter of the world's trees.

Synevyr National Nature Park, Zakarpattia Oblast, Ukraine

Dawn breaks over the Carpathians in southwest Ukraine. The trees here range from beeches that turn golden in autumn, to firs and spruces at higher altitudes, with some dwarf alder and juniper at the highest elevations. The park is home to brown bears and wolves.

Pripyat, Ukraine

Built to house the workers of the nearby Chernobyl Nuclear Power Station, the city of Pripyat had a population of about 50,000 people when a reactor at the power station exploded in April 1986. Within days the residents were evacuated, never to return. A 30km (19 mile) exclusion zone was set up around Chernobyl and, decades later, this remains the most radioactive environment on the planet. In the months after the explosion, wildlife and pine forest in the surrounding area died off, but, within a few seasons, and benefiting from the absence of human activity, wolves, beavers and lynx, among other animals, began to return to the forest and the abandoned farmland. Today 70 per cent of the zone is largely birch, maple and poplar forest. In Pripyat itself, the trees have grown up and closed in on the apartment blocks. It is estimated that it will take another 270 years for the radiation to fall to safe levels.

RIGHT TOP AND BOTTOM:
Cozia, Vâlcea County, Romania

Located in the southern Carpathians, Cozia is one of the mountain range's ancient forests. Chamois, deer and wildcats can be spotted here. American liverwort (*Hepatica americana*) (pictured) is one of the first flowers to bloom in spring.

FAR RIGHT:
Letea, Tulcea County, Romania

The fall of Nicolae Ceausescu in 1989 didn't just spell the end of Communist rule in Romania and its first free elections, it also meant freedom for a number of horses. With the closure of the country's collective farms, some horses were released into the wild and joined the existing feral population in Letea Forest. This has now swelled to more than 2,000 horses. Situated between branches of the Danube Delta, Letea is the northern-most subtropical forest in Europe.

RIGHT:
**Logging in Frakto,
Rhodope, Greece**
Frakto lies on the northern
Greek-Bulgarian border in
the Rhodope Mountains.
An ancient forest, some of
its trees are more than 300
years old. Managed logging
does continue in the area,
but, in part because of its
remoteness, illegal logging
and deforestation is not a
concern here.

OPPOSITE LEFT:
Frakto, Rhodope, Greece
With the decrease in sheep
herding and depopulation of
the area around Frakto during
the 20th century, the trees,
including Norway spruce
(*Picea abies*) and silver birch
(*Betula pendula*), have thrived.

OPPOSITE RIGHT:
**Mount Ida, Balıkesir
Çanakkale Province, Turkey**
Described by Homer as the
location where the Olympian
Gods gathered to watch the
Trojan War, Mount Ida is now
the battleground between a
Canadian mining company
and protestors – the felling
of 200,000 trees began in
2017. It has also been claimed
that thousands of tonnes of
cyanide have been used in
the extraction of gold, thus
risking the contamination of
local water supplies.

ALL PHOTOGRAPHS:
Julian Alps, Slovenia
The Julian Alps are a southern limestone mountain range that stretches from northern Slovenia across to northeastern Italy. In 2003, UNESCO included the Julian Alps and the Triglav National Park, which covers much of this area, in the international network of biosphere reserves.

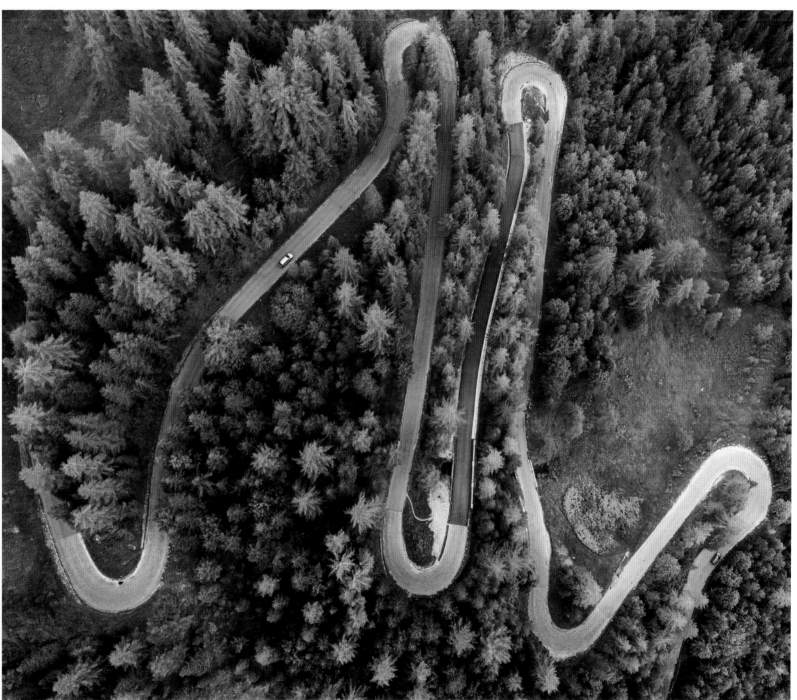

OPPOSITE:

Plitvice Lakes National Park, Croatia

The chain of 16 terraced lakes at Plitvice was formed by river water flowing over limestone and chalk, gradually depositing limestone to make dams. This raises the water level, creating lakes, caves and waterfalls. The upper lakes are surrounded by dense forest.

FAR LEFT:

Vizzavona, Haute-Corse, Corsica

Corsican pine bark in Vizzavona's pine and beech forest. Vizzavona is known for its Corsican pines (*Pinus nigra subsp. laricio*), which only grow naturally on the island. This hardy tree with silvery-grey bark is suited to rocky soil, doesn't require much water and can grow up to 40m (131ft) tall.

LEFT:

Valle Vigezzo, Piedmont, Italy

Tucked beneath the Swiss border, the Valle Vigezzo is unusual in that it has two rivers flowing through it. One flows west towards the Toce River; the other east towards Lake Maggiore.

'I have discovered a scent that reminds me of a spring morning in Italy, of mountain narcissus, orange blossom just after the rain,' wrote Vigezzo-born Giovanni Maria Farina in 1708. He named his scent after the German city he'd moved to – Cologne.

ALL PHOTOGRAPHS:

**Belluno Dolomites,
Veneto, Italy**
Located in northeastern Italy, the Dolomites (far left) form part of the southern Limestone Alps.

While the Italians and French call the flower pictured top left the 'Star of the Alps', and the Romanians call it 'Cliffhanger's flower', its Latin name *Leontopodium nivale* means the 'lion's paw'. But it is best known in English by its German name: Edelweiss ('noble white'). It blooms between July and September.

The harebell (*Campanula rotundifolia*) (bottom left), or Scottish bluebell, is found across the northern hemisphere. It flowers in late summer and autumn.

Sila National Park, Calabria, Italy
In season, Sila is a popular place for picking chestnuts, berries and porcini mushrooms (*Boletus edulis*). The forest is known for its black pines (*Pinus nigra*), white spruce (*Picea glauca*) and beech trees.

FAR RIGHT:
Stelvio National Park, Trentino-Alto Adige-Südtirol, and Lombardy, Italy
Situated in the heart of the Central Alps, Stelvio is home to roe deer, chamois and ibex, along with grouse and golden eagles (*Aquila chrysaetos*). Flora include the glacier buttercup (*Ranunculus glacialis*) and snowbell (*Soldanella pusilla*).

FAR LEFT:

Ordesa y Monte Perdido National Park, Aragon, Spain

Ranging from 700–3,000m (2,300–9,840ft), the spectacular Ordesa y Monte Perdido National Park is in the Aragonese province of Huesca in the Pyrenees. The pine and beech trees give way at higher altitudes to alpine pastures. Brown bears and bearded vultures can be seen. Pictured is the Añisclo Canyon, which has been carved into the limestone by the Bellós River running down from Monte Perdido.

LEFT:

Anaga Mountains, Tenerife, Canary Islands, Spain

The Anaga Mountains are known for their laurel forest (laurasilva), a type of subtropical forest characterised by broadleaf but evergreen tree species, such as (but not always) members of the laurel family (Lauraceae). Laurel forests are noted for their diversity of species.

LEFT:

Otzarreta, Parque Natural de Gorbeia, Basque Country, Spain

Unusually, the branches of the 100 beech trees at Otzarreta grow up rather than out. When they were about 50 years old, the trunks of these trees were cut at about 3m (10ft) by woodsman for charcoal production. The branches that grew back rose vertically.

ABOVE:

Garajonay National Park, La Gomera, Canary Islands, Spain

Three million years ago, almost all of southern Europe was covered in subtropical laurel forest like this one. Laurel trees in these forests have adapted to the more humid environment by growing waxier leaves, which repel water. Ferns can be seen on the ground.

RIGHT:

Irati, Navarre, Spain

Covering 17,300 hectares (42,800 acres), Irati is a large beech and fir forest in the western Pyrenees. Relatively isolated, Irati's environments range from forests to wetlands, and from subalpine meadows to Atlantic heaths.

OPPOSITE:

Alentejo Cork Forest, Portugal

Portugal is the world's largest producer of cork, used not only for wine bottles, but in flooring, shoes and in musical instruments. It takes 25 years for cork oak (*Quercus suber*) to reach a big enough size for bark to be taken. Cork can then be harvested by axe every eight to 11 years, and will be productive for about 150 years.

Africa and the Middle East

Asked to picture a forest in Africa, we might imagine a mountainous rainforest teeming with wildlife and not a human face to be seen for miles around. But is that what forests are really like? The flora and fauna, we argue, must be protected, but where does that leave the people who live or work in forests, and have done so for centuries? In creating reserves, governments and conservationists pushed the semi-nomadic Bayaka people in the Republic of the Congo and the Batwa in Uganda off the land they had lived on for hundreds of years. And perhaps, more than the governments and scientists, they were the people who understood the forest best in the first place.

Wars can be fought in forests and they can even be fought over them. Forests can become a refuge for people fleeing a conflict and the woods can reclaim abandoned lands when the fighting's done and the battle has moved on. But in Liberia in the 1990s, wood itself became the currency that funded much of the civil war. In a poor country with a wealth of raw material in wood, it was the 'logs of war', as they became known, that were being exported in exchange for arms.

Lastly, how forested does a forest need to be in order to be called that? The dry, sparse woodland of the Quiver Tree Forest in Namibia might make us redefine our ideas.

OPPOSITE:
Dragon's Blood Forest, Socotra, Yemen
Lying 380km (240 miles) south of the Arabian peninsula, the Socotra archipelago has developed a unique flora. Thirty-seven per cent of its plant species, including the dragon's blood tree (*Dracaena cinnabari*), are found nowhere else. The tree is named for its blood-red sap.

RIGHT:

Barbary macaque, Cèdre Gouraud Forest, Azrou, Morocco
Native to the Atlas Mountains, Barbary macaques (*Macaca sylvanus*) can be found among the cedar trees of the Cèdre Gouraud Forest. A protected species in Morocco and Algeria, the macaques' greatest threat is habitat loss, mainly from logging, which forces them to retreat higher into the mountains, where food – fruits, seeds, roots, fungi and occasionally frogs and tadpoles – is less plentiful. Barbary macaques are listed as endangered by the International Union for Conservation of Nature (IUCN).

OPPOSITE:

Cork forest, Jendouba Governorate, Tunisia
Located in the Kroumirie Mountains in northwestern Tunisia, this cork forest provides the only suitable habitat for Barbary deer (*Cervus elaphus barbarus*), Africa's only native deer. The best cork is used to make bottle stoppers. Lesser, cheaper cork is used in shoes or furniture.

Mount Cameroon, Southwest Region, Cameroon

An active volcano, Mount Cameroon rises from sea level to 4,040m (13,250ft). Its vegetation varies from lowland rainforests of evergreen trees, to cloud forests, to open-canopied forests, before reaching scrub and grassland at higher altitudes. The mountain is home to more than 100 African forest elephants (*Loxodonta cyclotis*).

RIGHT:

Sapo National Park, Sinoe County, Liberia

Sapo National Park contains the second-largest area of primary tropical rainforest in West Africa. Swamp forest, as pictured here, makes up 13 per cent of Sapo. Some trees grow up to 70m (230ft) tall.

FAR RIGHT:

Fern, Yekepa, Nimba County, Liberia

The bud of a fern frond in a forest in Liberia's northeast. The country's forests are in better health now than during Liberia's civil war in the 1990s, when selling rights to log the rainforests – the 'logs of war' as they became known – paid for the various factions' guns. At one point, 86 per cent of the country's timber production was controlled by arms traders.

Salonga National Park, Democratic Republic of Congo
In 1999, Salonga National Park was labelled as endangered on the UNESCO World Heritage List because of poaching and construction. However, subsequent conservation efforts meant that in 2021 the park's endangered status was removed. There are no roads in the park, which covers 3.6 million hectares (8.9 million acres). Most of the rainforest is accessible only by river, and within its rich ecosystem are leopards, bongo antelopes (*Tragelaphus eurycerus*) and bonobos (*Pan paniscus*) (below).

ALL PHOTOGRAPHS:

Quiver Tree Forest, Namibia
The rock hyrax (*Procavia capensis*) (right) is found across most of sub-Saharan Africa and the Middle East. Although it is at most 50cm (20in) long and weighs around 4kg (8.8lb), its closest living land relative is the elephant. The similarity between the two can be seen in their teeth, toes and skull structures.

The San people traditionally used the branches of the quiver tree (*Aloidendron dichotomum*) to make quivers (far right). This forest of about 250 quiver trees is one of the few to have grown spontaneously.

OPPOSITE:

Newlands, Western Cape, South Africa
Part of the Table Mountain National Park, Newlands has changed a great deal in the past 150 years. Originally a Southern Afrotemperate Forest with tall trees, shade and layers of different species, logging in the 19th century led to replanting of much of the area with commercial pine plantations.

BELOW:

oNgoye Hills Forest Reserve, KwaZulu-Natal, South Africa
Ten kilometres (six miles) inland from the Indian Ocean, this patch of transitional Afromontane-coastal forest is home to such rare species as the oNgoye dwarf cyclad (*Encephalartos ngoyanus*), Pondo fig (*Ficus bizanae*) and the Natal elm (*Celtis mildbraedii*).

FAR LEFT, ABOVE AND LEFT:
Amani Nature Reserve, Tango Region, Tanzania
Located in the East Amani Usambara Mountains, this reserve is a mix of tropical submontane, lowland and plantation forests. In it are the Nest Fern (*Asplenium* sp.) (above), and the Peacock Tree Frog (*Leptopelis vermiculatus*) (left).

OPPOSITE:
Selous Game Reserve, Tanzania
In Selous in 2014, there were 13,000 African bush elephants (*Loxodonta africana*). While that may seem a lot, in 1976 there were 109,000. Poachers and corrupt officials have been blamed for their decline.

Masoala National Park, Madagascar

Masoala features both lowland, coastal and flooded forests, as well as marsh and mangrove. Despite being a national park, Masoala was still invaded by illegal loggers in 2009–10 looking for rosewood. On the other hand, local farmers argue that when the park was created in 1997, they lost access to some of their farming land.

Pitcher Plant, Atsinanana, Madagascar

A type of carnivorous plant found mainly in southeast Asia, this species, *Nepenthes madagascariensis*, is native to Madagascar. The plant's pitcher contains a viscous fluid that drowns insects that fall inside, before absorbing their nutrients. The 'lid' on top of the plant limits rainfall from diluting the fluid within the pitcher.

Mau, Kenya
In 2009, it was reported that a quarter of the Mau Forest had been lost over a 15-year period. The finger was pointed at corrupt politicians who licensed deforestation to create farmland – largely for tea and wheat production – for their constituents and friends. But deforestation doesn't just mean fewer trees. The forests capture moisture blowing in off the Indian Ocean and release it into the rivers. In this photograph, forest trees have been replaced with plantation conifers.

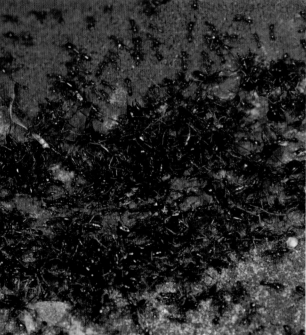

ALL PHOTOGRAPHS:

**Arabuko Sokoke,
Coast Province, Kenya**

Yellow baboons (*Papio cynocephalus*) (opposite left) are found in light forests and savannahs across east Africa from Kenya down to Zimbabwe. Apart from forests, Arabuko Sokoke is also home to wetlands (opposite right) and tidal creeks.

The Arabuko Sokoke Forest is also noted for the high number of species not found anywhere else, such as the golden-rumped elephant shrew (*Rhynchocyon chrysopygus*) (far left top), which is, in fact, more closely related to elephants, such as the African Bush elephant (*Loxodonta Africana*) (left), than to shrews.

The jaws of the Siafu ant (*Dorylus* genus) (far bottom left) are so strong that it won't release its hold even if pulled in two. The Maasai people turn this to their advantage. If they suffer a bad cut while in the bush, they will get a soldier Siafu to bite on each side of the gash, then break off the body. The fixed jaws create a temporary stitch.

81

ALL PHOTOGRAPHS:

Bwindi Impenetrable Forest, Kanungu District, Uganda
A primeval forest, Bwindi is 'impenetrable' because, originally, its dense hardwood, bamboo, ferns and vines made it difficult to cross. In 1991, the Bwindi Impenetrable National Park was established, in part to protect the forest's endangered species, including the mountain gorilla (*Gorilla beringei beringei*). Gorilla numbers have increased from an estimated 300 in 1997 to, according to a census in 2019, 459 gorillas – almost half the world's mountain gorilla population. But in creating the park, the local Batwa pygmy tribe was evicted and lost their hunting rights.

Budongo Forest Reserve, Uganda

Lianas (right) are vines that grow up around trees in tropical, deciduous rainforests. In general, they are detrimental to the trees that support them.

Mubende Witch Tree (*Pterygota mildbraedii*) (far right) is logged for firewood and to make charcoal. It can grow up to 40m (131ft) tall.

Dutchman's pipe (*Aristolochia elegans*) (opposite left) is a climbing vine that at times has been used as a medicinal plant to treat malaria and snake bites. It is pollinated by flies that are attracted to the carrion-like odour it emits. Whether or not of any medicinal use, it does contain Aristolochic acids, which can cause liver and kidney damage.

Uganda ironwood (*Cynometra alexandrii*) seed pods (opposite right). Humans and chimpanzees both like Uganda ironwood, the dominant tree species at Budongo. Humans use it for flooring and railway sleepers, while chimps like its bendy properties for making sleeping platforms each night.

OPPOSITE:

Dibeen, Jerash Governorate, Jordan

One of the Middle East's last remaining pine-oak forests, Dibeen begins with Aleppo pines (*Pinus halepensis*) at lower altitudes of 500m (1640ft), which mix with Palestine oaks (*Quercus calliprinos*) at mid-levels, before giving way to smaller Aleppo oak (*Quercus infectoria*) at higher levels of around 1,000m (3,280ft).

LEFT:

Al Shouf Cedar Nature Reserve, Mount Lebanon Governorate, Lebanon

The cedar forests of Lebanon feature in the ancient Mesopotamian poem *The Epic of Gilgamesh* – written between the third and first millennium BCE – making them the oldest documented forests in the world. Apart from cedars, there are also oaks, pines and junipers in the forest. Animals include the Nubrian ibex (*Capra nubiana*) and the Syrian brown bear (*Ursus arctos syriacus*).

ALL PHOTOGRAPHS:

Dragon's Blood Forest, Socotra, Yemen
Smaller quantities of the dragon's blood tree's berries are fed to goats, while for centuries the tree's red resin has been used as a dye. The tree's unusual shape is an adaptation to the arid climate and rocky terrain. The umbrella-like covering captures moisture, provides shade and reduces evaporation, allowing seeds to grow beneath adult trees. Classified as vulnerable, the species is suffering from overgrazing by goats, the impact of severe cyclones, and the gradual drying out of the archipelago.

Asia and the Pacific

In 1876, Henry Wickham smuggled thousands of seeds from Amazon rubber trees to Kew Gardens in London, where they were cultivated and later used to establish rubber plantations in Malaysia, displacing the existing forest. Similarly, the French set up rubber plantations in Indochina, while the Americans did the same in Liberia. Once the preserve of the Amazon, rubber was now produced in Africa and Asia.

Today we can see the devastation caused by logging, but we also know that trees are felled to make, for example, furniture for a global market, that the produce of oil palm plantations is used in soap, chocolate bars, animal feed and biofuels, and that plantations of eucalyptus trees provide us with paper pulp to make books.

Plantation owners may increasingly strive at sustainability, but they introduce new species that offer less canopy cover and reduced biodiversity – unlike a rainforest, they're growing just one plant. Orangutans are only found on the islands of Borneo and Sumatra and today three-quarters of their population – it's down to the tens of thousands – live on plantations.

Lastly, apart from industry, forests are also cultural or spiritual places. We may live in towns and cities, but we return to nature. Mount Kumgang has a strong cultural presence in Korean culture but is in North Korea. During a period of détente between North and South Korea, the mountain was the first place opened up for South Koreans to visit.

OPPOSITE:
Lake of Ghosts, Mazandaran, Iran
Located in the north of Iran near the Caspian Sea, the Lake of Ghosts is so named because of its half-submerged trees often shrouded in mist. The swampy lake's proper name is *Mamraz*, meaning 'hornbeam' (*Carpinus betulus*). While the hornbeams in the lake have suffered from being surrounded by water, the alders (*Alnus* genus) are suited to the wetland environment.

ALL PHOTOGRAPHS:

**Gir National Park and
Wildlife Sanctuary, Gujarat,
India**

Based around what
was once the Nawab of
Junagarh's hunting region,
the Gir National Park, a
dry, deciduous forest, was
established in 1965. Gir
and its surrounding area
is now the only natural
habitat where the Asiatic
lion (*Panthera leo leo*) is
found. Once ranging from
the Middle East to northern
India, the lion was hunted to
near extinction in India. By
the end of the 19th century
there were only about
100 Asiatic lions left. The
subspecies is still endangered,
but numbers have improved.

The chital (right), also
known as the spotted deer
(*Axis axis*), is native to the
Indian subcontinent.

ALL PHOTOGRAPHS:
Mollem National Park, Goa, India
The lower part of Dudhsagar Falls (right) on the Mandovi River in western India. Emerging from deciduous forests, the viaduct above carries a railway across the falls.

These forests, which include tropical evergreens, are important for providing a habitat for local species such as the Bonnet macaques (*Macaca radiata*) (opposite left) or Ashy drongo (*Dicrurus leucophaeus*) (opposite right). In addition to this, when the south-eastern Indian city of Chennai suffered a drought in 2019, scientists calculated that the city depended on 50 per cent of its rainfall from the forests of western India capturing rain and allowing it to evaporate back into the atmosphere. But 35 per cent of those forests have been lost over the past century.

ALL PHOTOGRAPHS:
**Sinharaja Forest Reserve,
Sabaragamuwa and
Southern Provinces,
Sri Lanka**
With 240,000 plants per
hectare (100,000 per acre),
Sinharaja is the most densely
vegetated rainforest in Asia.
Located in southwest Sri
Lanka, the lowland, virgin
rainforest – the island's last
surviving one – is home to
at least 139 endemic plant
species and 95 per cent of
Sri Lanka's endemic bird
species, as well as the Indian
chameleon (*Chamaeleo
zeylanicus*) (opposite left),
the only chameleon found in
Asia, and the golden orb-
weaver spider (*Nephila* genus)
(opposite right).

Sinharaja's rare endemic
trees include the palm
Loxococcus rupicola. The
reserve is threatened by illegal
logging and agrochemicals
from neighbouring tea
plantations polluting the
shared rivers and streams.

Jiuzhaigou Valley, Sichuan, China

Situated in the Min Mountains on the edge of the Tibetan Plateau in southwestern China, the Jiuzhaigou Nature Reserve is known for its 100 clear-water lakes, where mineral deposits colour the water blue, green or turquoise. The jagged mountains are forested with a mix of broadleaf and coniferous trees.

Changbai Mountains, Jilin Province, China
On China's border with North Korea, the Changbai Mountains feature mixed forests of both deciduous and coniferous trees. At the top of the tree line are mountain birches and larches, while lower down spruce, fir and pine trees can be found, with maple, elm and lime trees at the lowest altitudes.

Changbai Mountains, Jilin Province, China
Rangers patrol a tree farm in a forest reserve. The remote forests of the Changbai Mountains are home to the Siberian tiger (*Panthera tigris tigris*), an endangered species, as well as vulnerable species such as the Siberian musk deer (*Moschus moschiferus*) and the Asiatic black bear (*Ursus thibetanus*). Threats to the area include illegal hunting, deforestation and the exploitation of medicinal plants, such as ginseng.

OPPOSITE:
Mount Kumgang, Kangwon-do, North Korea
Also known as Diamond Mountain, Mount Kumgang has for centuries had immense cultural significance in Korean art and poetry, but when the country divided, the mountain ended up in the North and South Koreans were no longer able to visit it. But in 1998, visitors were allowed from the South, as part of an effort to promote reconciliation between the two countries. Tours to the region, however, came to an abrupt end in 2008 when a North Korean soldier shot dead a South Korean tourist who had strayed from the path.

LEFT:

Odaesan National Park, Gangwon-do, South Korea

Korea's densest and lushest forest, Odaesan National Park is named after Mount Odaesan, a sacred mountain in Korean Buddhism. The mountain not only houses archives of the Joseon Dynasty (14th–19th century), but also three Buddhist temples and hermitages. Some of the park's fir trees are 600 years old.

RIGHT:

Tadasu no Mori, Shimogamo Jinja, Kyoto, Japan

Tadasu no Mori, the 'Forest of Correction', is a 12-hectare (30-acre) sacred grove of virgin forest now in the grounds of the Shimogamo Shinto Shrine in the city of Kyoto. The forest trees are not managed and, apart from damage from fires or war, have been allowed to grow in their natural way.

Aokigahara, Mount Fuji, Yamanashi, Japan
Situated on Mount Fuji's northwestern flank, the broadleaf and conifer trees in Aokigahara Forest benefit from the forest floor's volcanic rock. Up to an elevation of 1,800m (5,900ft), Aokigahara's most dominant tree species is a conifer – the northern Japanese hemlock (*Tsuga diversifolia*). At higher altitudes, the most populous tree is Veitch's silver-fir (*Abies veitchii*).

Aokigahara, which means 'blue tree meadow', has long been associated with *yurei* – ghostly spirits in Japanese folklore – and in the past 50 years has sadly become one of the world's most-used suicide sites.

**Arashiyama Forest,
Kyoto Prefecture, Japan**

The whistling of the wind
through the trees, the
tapping of the trunks as they
knock together, the creak
of the bending wood and
the rustling of the bamboo
branch leaves earned the
Arashiyama Forest a place on
the Japanese government's
'100 Soundscapes' initiative
to motivate people to leave
their homes and enjoy some
fresh air. When the pathways
aren't too busy, the denseness
of the swaying trees and
sound can make Arashiyama
a meditative place.

But Arashiyama isn't
remote at all; it's on the
outskirts of the city of Kyoto.
Also known as the Sagano
Bamboo Forest, Arashiyama
covers 16 sq km (6 sq miles)
of largely Moso bamboo
(*Phyllostachys edulis*). The
species is native to China
and Taiwan and can reach
up to 28m (92ft) tall. It is
the species most commonly
used in the bamboo textile
industry, such as in the
production of rayon.

ALL PHOTOGRAPHS:

Cardamom Mountains, Cambodia

Sparsely populated, the Cardamom Mountains straddle Cambodia's southwestern border with Thailand. The western slopes on the Thai side are a dense rainforest with more than 380cm (150in) of rain a year. The mountain's rain shadow means that the eastern slopes on the Cambodian side receive a third less rain.

Cardamon and pepper are commercially farmed on the eastern slopes. The illegal logging of rosewood, often transported through Vietnam and on to China to make antique-style furniture, has been a problem in the mountains.

Reptiles found here include Flower's long-headed lizard (*Pseudocalotes floweri*) and, pictured above, the oriental garden lizard (*Calotes versicolor*).

Ba Be National Park, Bac Kan Province, Vietnam

Ba Be – 'Three Lakes' – is surrounded by towering limestone outcrops, caves and evergreen forests. At 8km (5 miles) long and 150m (492ft) above sea level, it is Vietnam's largest and highest freshwater lake. During the dry season (November–May), the lake drains into the Nang River, but during the wet season (May–November) the flow is reversed and the river flows into the lake. Among the animals found in the park are the Chinese pangolin (*Manis pentadactyla*) and the Vietnamese salamander (*Paramesotriton deloustali*). One of its dominant tree species is the rare *Burretiodendron hsienmu*, which the local Tay people use for building stilt houses.

ALL PHOTOGRAPHS:
Cát Bà Island, Vietnam
Cát Bà Island and the numerous, smaller neighbouring islands in Ha Long Bay are known for their steep, evergreen limestone cliffs which plunge into the South China Sea where the boats of pearl and shrimp fishermen cluster around floating villages. On land, there is mangrove forest and, higher up, tropical rainforest (right).

One of the rarest primates in the world, the Cát Bà langur (*Trachypithecus poliocephalus*) (left) is a critically endangered species endemic to Cát Bà Island. Illegal poaching for use in traditional medicine, plus habitat fragmentation caused by the huge growth in tourism in the area, has reduced numbers from more than 2,000 during the 1960s to a low of 53 by the year 2000. By 2020, numbers had risen to more than 65.

ALL PHOTOGRAPHS:

Khao Sok National Park, Surat Thani, Thailand
Also known as Rajjaprabha Dam Reservoir, Cheow Lan Lake (opposite) is a 185 sq km (71 sq mile) artificial lake created in 1987 when the Rajjaprabha Dam was completed. The dam serves as a hydro-electric power station, and to manage flooding and irrigation. In flooding the area, 385 villagers had to be resettled, each family given financial compensation and 2.9 hectares (7.2 acres) of rubber plantation to manage. With more than 200 plant species per hectare (83 per acre), Khao Sok is one of the most biodiverse places on the planet.

ALL PHOTOGRAPHS:

Khao Sok National Park, Surat Thani, Thailand
Khao Sok is estimated to contain more than five per cent of the world's species. Among the mammals are the Malayan tapir (*Acrocodia indica*) and Asian elephant (*Elephas maximus*). Found in the park and across south and southeast Asia, the reticulated python (*Malayopython reticulatus*) (opposite) is a non-venomous constrictor.

Possibly the world's largest flower, the endangered species *Rafflesia kerrii* (left) is only found in this part of Thailand and in Malaysia. Usually 50–90cm (19.5–35.5in) in diameter, the flower stinks of rotten meat – a way of attracting pollinator insects. It is a parasite of vines and beneath the flower a network of fibres will penetrate the host plant, such as an Indian chestnut vine (*Tetrastigma leucostaphylum*).

ALL PHOTOGRAPHS:

Kinabalu National Park, Sabah, Malaysian Borneo, Malaysia

Kinabulu National Park ranges over four climate zones, from tropical lowland rainforest to montane oak, up to coniferous forests and finally reaching alpine meadows. On Mount Kinabulu itself, there are more than 5,000 plant species, excluding mosses and liverworts. It has been suggested that this huge diversity is due to the immense climatic range from sea level to mountain, and that the mountain's elevation – 4,095m (13,435ft) at its peak – provided refuge to species adapted to the cold during interglacial periods.

Mount Kinabulu is home to more than 600 species of fern – more than the whole of Africa – including the Mountain tree fern *Cyathea contaminans* (right top) and 50 species that are found nowhere else. The mountain is also known for 13 species of carnivorous *Nepenthes* pitcher plants (right bottom), five of which are endemic to the forest. The prey, often insects, fall into the pitfall traps, where they drown in the plant's digestive fluids.

ALL PHOTOGRAPHS:

Danum Valley, Sabah, Malaysian Borneo, Malaysia
Located in the far northeast of Borneo, the Danum Valley
Conservation Area is made up of largely primary lowland
rainforest. Today, there are controlled visitor tours, but before
the 1990s this remote area was entirely uninhabited. The forest
consists of predominantly Dipterocarpus tree species, such as
Dipterocarpus turbinatus, which is sold as Keruing timber.

Animal species include the Horsfield's tarsier (*Cephalopachus
bancanus*), the endangered Borneo pygmy elephant and,
pictured above, the venomous Lichen Huntsman Spider
(*Heteropoda boiei*), a species native to Borneo and Sumatra.

LEFT:

Rainforest and oil palm plantation, Sarawak, Malaysian Borneo, Malaysia

A rainforest gives way to an oil palm plantation. Oil palm is used as a butter substitute, a foaming agent in soap, and in biofuels. In recent decades, the Malaysian state of Sarawak, which is almost as big as England, has become the world's biggest supplier of logs used for furniture, panelling and plywood. But as the World Bank reported during the 1990s, Sarawak's logging was 'a sunset industry'. The trees weren't being replanted and were going to run out. Today, only five per cent of the state's primary forest remains.

RIGHT:

The Batang Ai National Park, Sarawak, Malaysian Borneo, Malaysia

A Cup fungus (*Cookeina tricholoma*). Water collects in the funnel-shaped cup and is absorbed into the fungus. When the water level drops due to evaporation, the cells inside the fungus dry out, break through the tissue wall and release the spores.

Taman Negara, Malaysia

One of the world's oldest deciduous rainforests – estimates stretch up to 130 million years – Taman Negara (meaning 'National Park' in Malay) was given protected status in 1938.

The Batang Ai National Park, Sarawak, Malaysian Borneo, Malaysia

The Batang Ai National Park consists of 24 sq km (9.3 sq miles) of tropical rainforest, created when the area was flooded to make a hydro-electric reservoir. Orangutans and gibbons live in the forest but flooding also displaced local Iban people.

ALL PHOTOGRAPHS:

Taman Negara, Malaysia
Stretching across an area of 4,343 sq km (1,677 sq miles), Malaysia's national park includes 10,000 plant species, 150,000 insect species, 270 reptile species, 250 freshwater fish species, 200 mammal species, 675 bird species, including the orange-backed woodpecker (*Chrysocolaptes validus*) (opposite top right), and 25,000 invertebrate species, including the stinging slug caterpillar (opposite bottom right).

Rare species found in the park include the critically endangered Malay tiger (*Panthera tigris tigris* subspecies) and the Malayan gaur (*Bos gaurus*), as well as the Malayan peacock-pheasant (*Polyplectron malacense*).

It is estimated that there are on average more than 200 different tree species per hectare in Taman Negara.

Female Sumatran orangutan, Bukit Lawang, North Sumatra, Indonesia

Orangutan means 'person of the forest' in Malay. Bukit Lawang is the largest animal sanctuary of the Sumatran orangutan (*Pongo abelii*), a critically endangered species found only in the forests on the island of Sumatra.

In recent years, the sanctuary has successfully rehabilitated orangutans displaced by logging and habitat loss. Its forest area is now at saturation point and the sanctuary can no longer accept any orphaned orangutans. The species has a naturally low population density with a large home range – up to 24km (15 miles) for a male – as it needs to move from lowland to intermediate to highland forest regions seasonally in search of fruit.

Forest, North Sumatra, Indonesia

Forests absorb 25 to 30 per cent of the extra carbon dioxide being pumped into the air by humans. The air in the forest in Sumatra can be up to 10 degrees Celsius (18 degrees Fahrenheit) cooler than in neighbouring, newly planted, palm oil plantations.

**Mahakam River,
East Kalimantan,
Borneo, Indonesia**
In 2018, forests covered just
under half of Indonesia's land
area. But just 70 years earlier,
in 1950, forests had covered
87 per cent of the country.
Meranti and other rainforest
trees in East Kalimantan are
felled for the timber industry.
Logging, much of it illegal,
and the burning of forests
to make way for agriculture,
have made Indonesia, after
China and the USA, the
world's third largest emitter
of greenhouse gases.

**Meratus Mountains,
South Kalimantan,
Borneo, Indonesia**
Logging in forests
doesn't necessarily mean
deforestation. Trees can be
replanted and, even if they
aren't replanted, if the land
isn't exhausted and the area
not so large that the local
climate has changed, seeds
will fall and new trees
will grow.

LEFT:

Papua New Guinea
Almost 70 per cent of Papua
New Guinea is covered
in lowland or montane
rainforest but, from the year
2000 to 2020, the total area
of humid primary forest in
Papua New Guinea decreased
by 2.4 per cent. Trees are
felled for timber and replaced
with plantations, or the
cleared land is used for
agriculture.

RIGHT:

**Central Range montane
rainforests, Papua New
Guinea**
The flora and fauna of the
island of New Guinea is a mix
of tropical rainforest species
found within Asia and those
found in Australia. Marsupials
such as the endangered
Matschie's tree-kangaroo
(*Dendrolagus matschiei*) live
in the forests of Papua New
Guinea's Central Range.

ALL PHOTOGRAPHS.

Daintree National Park, Queensland, Australia

Daintree is part of the Wet Tropics of Queensland Rainforest, the oldest continually surviving tropical rainforest in the world. It is one of the few places in the world where a rainforest runs down to sandy beaches and to a reef – in this case, the Great Barrier Reef.

In September 2021, the deeds to more than 160,000 hectares (395,000 acres) of northern Queensland territory, encompassing Daintree National Park, were given to the Aboriginal Australian Eastern Kuku Yalanki people, who now jointly manage the park with the Queensland government.

The leaves of the Australian fan palm (*Licuala ramsayi*) (far left), which is native to northern Queensland, grow up to 2m (6ft) long and form a near perfect circle. The palm's fruits are eaten by the southern cassowary bird (*Casuarius casuarius*); the tree's leaves can be used for thatch and food wrapping.

The Ixora shield bug (*Catacanthus punctus*) (top right) is native to Australia. It can be found on spur mahogany trees (*Dysoxylum pettigrewianum*).

Boyd's Forest Dragon (*Hypsilurus boydii*) (bottom right), an arboreal lizard, is only found in the Wet Tropics of northern Queensland.

ALL PHOTOGRAPHS:

K'gari (Fraser Island), Queensland, Australia

At 1,840 sq km (710 sq miles), K'gari (Fraser Island) is possibly the largest sand island in the world. It was created by sand pushed by sea currents and accumulating on volcanic bedrock. Unlike many sand dunes, plant life is abundant on the island because the sand carried with it fungi which can be absorbed – and so feed – plant life.

K'gari is covered in rainforest, mangrove forest, swamplands, eucalyptus woodlands and heathland, which can be susceptible to bush fires (opposite). From the 1860s to 1991, logging was one of the island's industries. Being resistant to marine boring invertebrates, satinay (*Syncarpia hillii*) trees, part of the myrtle family, were logged here during the 1860s and shipped to Egypt in the construction of the Suez Canal.

Horsehoe Falls, Mount Field National Park, Tasmania, Australia

Some 289 species of fungus have been recorded in the eucalyptus temperate rainforest and higher in the alpine moorland of the Mount Field National Park. While there are two destructive fungi species in the park, most are beneficial, breaking down fallen branches and leaf litter, freeing up the nutrients to be used by other organisms. Some fungi, such as the *Lacccaria* fungus (pictured top right), which often grows on Tasmanian myrtle beech (*Nothofagus cunninghamii*), have a symbiotic relationship with their host plant.

Mosses (bottom right) function like sponges, soaking up rainfall and holding on to water in the soil. In hot environments, they protect tree roots by offering shade.

**Coromandel Forest Park,
Waikato Region,
North Island, New Zealand**
Having evolved in isolation
for so long, the flora of New
Zealand is unique. Today, 80
per cent of the trees, ferns
and plants found there don't
grow anywhere else.

Once exploited for timber,
gold and Kauri tree gum, the
land and vegetation of the
Coromandel is today showing
signs of recovery.

LEFT AND OPPOSITE RIGHT:
Coromandel Peninsula, North Island, New Zealand
The Coromandel ranges from conifer and broadleaf rainforest up to subalpine plants at higher levels. Canopy trees include conifers such as rimu (*Dacrydium cupressinum*). Loggers made use of the V-shaped valleys and fast-flowing rivers, damming the waterways and then releasing the water to create a surge to carry logs down to tramways or rivermouths.

OPPOSITE FAR RIGHT:
Kauri trees, Waipoua Forest, North Island, New Zealand
The Kauri (*Agathis australis*) is one of the world's most ancient tree species. In the 19th century, Europeans heavily exploited Kauri, making use of the wood's elasticity and length to make ship's hulls, as well as houses and furniture.

Waipoua Forest, Northland Region, North Island, New Zealand

With diameters in excess of 5m (16ft) and reaching up to 50m (164ft) tall, the Kauri tree (*Agathis australis*) (above) is New Zealand's largest tree by volume.

This Kauri tree (far right), Tane Mahuta – 'Lord of the Forest' – is thought to be between 1,250 and 2,500 years old.

In Waipoua, the largest trees host epiphytes (right), which are plants that grow on other plants but aren't parasitic.

North America

In 1756, 21-year-old John Adams, the Massachusetts-born Founding Father to-be, but at the time just a graduate working as a schoolteacher, wrote in his diary that the American landscape was 'one continued dismal wilderness', and that the forests should be removed, 'the land covered with fields of corn, orchards bending with fruit, and magnificent habitations of rational and civilised people'. From Canada to Mexico, vast swathes of forests were cut down and converted into pasture, plantations or urban developments. In the early 20th century, efforts began to protect forestland in the United States. Even so, when the Redwood National Park in California was created in the 1960s, only 10 per cent of the old growth trees remained. Everything else had been logged. And with lower rainfall and higher temperatures, recent years have seen worsening forest fires on the Pacific Coast.

But in this chapter we also explore the forests that engulfed Mayan ruins in Mexico, so much so that many abandoned Mayan settlements are still buried, and, to an extent, preserved by the forest. When the people left, the trees reclaimed the land. Likewise, in parts of the United States where a decline in demand for land to grow crops has occurred, trees have re-emerged. Like Europe, North America is now more wooded than it was 150 years ago.

OPPOSITE:
Carmanah Walbran Provincial Park, Vancouver Island, British Columbia, Canada
Carmanah Walbran Provincial Park is known for primeval forests with immense Sitka spruces (*Picea sitchensis*) that grow along its riversides, as well as other coniferous species, such as Pacific red cedar (*Thuja plicata*).

ALL PHOTOGRAPHS:

Cathedral Grove, Macmillan Provincial Park, Vancouver Island, British Columbia, Canada

Macmillan Provincial Park's Cathedral Grove is a 157-hectare (390-acre) stand of primeval Douglas fir (*Pseudotsuga menziesii*). Some of the trees could be more than 800 years old and many reach up to 9m (30ft) in circumference. The Douglas fir is not a true fir, but from the pine family. When Douglas firs are felled, they are used for timber-frame construction and smaller ones as Christmas trees. In 1944, logging industrialist HR MacMillan donated much of the land of the Cathedral Grove to the province of British Columbia.

RIGHT:

Logging, British Columbia, Canada

Some 60 per cent of British Columbia is forested land, of which 94 per cent is publicly owned. Within publicly owned and privately owned land, logging licenses can be granted. About 50,000 people in British Columbia work in forestry. Sawmills, however, are suffering from the trend to ship raw logs abroad to be processed overseas.

OPPOSITE LEFT AND RIGHT:

Great Bear Rainforest, British Columbia, Canada

The Great Bear Rainforest is one of the largest surviving temperate rainforests in the world. The primeval forest's dominant trees include the western red cedar and the Sitka spruce. Cougars, Sitka deer and grey wolves can be found there. Moss species in the rainforest date back 450 million years and have survived huge climate changes, including ice ages.

Only found in British Columbia, the spirit bear (opposite right) is a Kermode bear (*Ursus americanus kermodei*) that is white rather than black, like the rest of the species. Salmon can more easily detect the dark outline of a Kermode bear than a white spirit bear. Consequently, spirit bears catch more salmon per day than Kermode bears do.

ALL PHOTOGRAPHS:

Crowsnest Pass, British Columbia-Alberta, Canada

Crowsnest Pass is the southern-most route across the Canadian Rockies. Before European settlers arrived, First Nations peoples used the pass when migrating and for trade between the mountain cultures and the plains cultures to the East. The Crowsnest River (opposite) runs east from the Rockies down through Alberta. The woodland is a temperate coniferous forest of aspens, pines and spruces.

Although Europeans brought their species of sheep to North America in the 16th century, bighorn sheep (*Ovis canadensis*) (right) had been present in North America since the Pleistocene Era (750,000 years ago), when they crossed the Bering land bridge from Siberia to Alaska.

Gaff Point, Nova Scotia, Canada

Facing the Atlantic Ocean, the exposed forests on Nova Scotia's coastline mainly consist of white spruce (*Picea glauca*) and balsam fir (*Abies balsamea*), a popular species across North America, east of the Rockies. Balsam fir has been used for thousands of years by Native Americans for medicinal purposes and more recently has become a popular species for Christmas trees.

Highway 400, Happy Valley Forest, Ontario, Canada

Running north out of Toronto, Highway 400 cuts through the Happy Valley Forest on the Oak Ridges Moraine, a band of rolling hills and river valleys created 12,000 years ago by a retreating glacier. Although only 6.48 sq km (2.50 sq miles) in size, the Happy Valley Forest supports more than 100 bird species, including the near-threatened cerulean warbler (*Setophaga cerulea*).

**Skagway River, Tongass
National Forest, USA**
Originating at the Laughton
Glacier trailhead in British
Columbia, Canada, the
Skagway River flows
southwest across the border
into Alaska and down to
temperate rainforests on the
Pacific Coast.

**Mad River Valley,
Green Mountains,
Vermont, USA**
Vermont is named after its
mountains: v*erts monts* is
French for 'green mountains'.
Part of the northeast
Appalachians, the Green
Mountains are covered in
temperate broadleaf and
mixed forests. These look
particularly spectacular in
autumn when the maples,
oaks, and birches turn
beautiful yellow, brown and
bronze colours.

Hoh Rainforest, Olympic National Park, Washington, USA
Receiving more than 500cm (200in) of rainfall a year, the Hoh is the continental United States' wettest rainforest. Its dominant tree species are the Sitka spruce (*Picea sitchensis*) and western hemlock (*Tsuga heterophylla*), followed by deciduous trees such as bigleaf maple (*Acer macrophyllum*) and red alder (*Alnus rubra*).

ALL PHOTOGRAPHS:

Olympic National Park, Washington, USA

Animals living in the Olympic National Park (opposite) include black-tailed deer, a subspecies of mule deer (*Odocoileus hemionus*), Roosevelt elk (*Cervus canadensis roosevelti*) and black bears (*Ursus americanus*). The rainforest is home to many unique mosses (left) and lichen, such as the lettuce lichen (*Lobaria oregana*), which is eaten by deer and elk.

Bridger-Teton National Forest, Wyoming, USA
Located in the northern Rocky Mountains, the Bridger-Teton National Forest covers 14,000 sq km (8,700 sq miles). It is part of the Greater Yellowstone Ecosystem (it borders Yellowstone National Park). Of the 55,000 wild grizzly bears (*Ursus arctos horribilis*) in North America, about 600 live in the Yellowstone-Teton area.

167

RIGHT:

Sawtooth Lake, Sawtooth Wilderness, Idaho, USA

Not just a description, but a federally protected area, the Sawtooth Wilderness is an area of 87,852 hectares (217,088 acres) of land where no logging or mechanical equipment is permitted, including bicycles. Grey wolves (*Canis lupus*) were successfully reintroduced to the area in the 1990s.

OPPOSITE:

Coolidge Ghost Town, Beaverhead-Deerlodge National Forest, Montana, USA

This was a silver-mining town that boomed from 1913 for a decade. At its peak, Coolidge had a population of 350 people, with a telephone service, school, post office and electricity. A century on, the buildings are slowly being absorbed by the pine trees.

ALL PHOTOGRAPHS OVERLEAF:

Redwoods National Park, California, USA

When the Redwoods National Park was created in 1968, nearly 90 per cent of the original redwood trees had been logged. A century earlier, Native Americans had lived in the forest, tending and planting trees, but were pushed aside in the gold rush and by timber harvesters. Reaching up to 115.5m (379ft), the coast redwood (*Sequoia sempervirens*) is the tallest tree species in the world.

Sequoia National Forest, California, USA
Climate change in California has seen lower rainfall, lower snowpack, higher temperatures and more wildfires in recent years. From March to October 2021, there was no rainfall in California at all. To fight wildfires, aircraft release fire retardant (below), a combination of water and fertiliser, which helps the water cling to plant material and repel flames. It is estimated that more than 1,000 giant sequoia trees (right) were destroyed in the forest fire in Kern County in August 2021.

ALL PHOTOGRAPHS:

**Saguaro Cactus Forest,
Saguaro National Park,
Arizona, USA**

The Saguaro National Park was established in 1994 to protect the fauna and flora of the area, including the giant saguaro cactus (*Carnegiea gigantea*), which can grow up to 12m (40ft) tall. The cactus is native to Arizona, as well as parts of California and the Mexican state of Sonora. Saguaro often live for more than 150 years and might produce their first side arm only after 70 years.

The Tohono O'odham and Pima Native American people have long used the cactus's fruits for making syrup and its inner ribs as building materials. Adapted to arid conditions, the plant's stomata – leaf pores – are closed during the day to avoid excessive evaporation, but open at night to absorb carbon dioxide.

LEFT:

Kelp Forest, Catalina Island, California, USA
Termed by some scientists 'the sequoias of the seas', kelp (brown algae seaweeds) absorb carbon dioxide – thereby reducing the acidification of the oceans – and release oxygen into the water.

ABOVE:

Rainbow Eucalyptus, Maui, Hawaii, USA
The only eucalyptus species to grow in rainforests, the rainbow eucalyptus (*Eucalyptus deglupta*) is native to Indonesia, the Philippines and New Guinea. It is also grown in plantations for pulpwood used in making paper.

ABOVE:

Pinyon pine, Humboldt-Toiyabe National Forest, Nevada, USA

The pinyon group of pines grows across the southwestern United States. Although all pines produce edible seeds (pine nuts), those of the pinyon are particularly nutritious and have long been a staple of Native Americans.

RIGHT:

Four Peaks Mountain, Tonto National Forest, Arizona, USA

Brush and pine-covered hillsides lead up to the Four Peaks Mountain, part of the Mazatzal Mountains in south-central Arizona. The vegetation ranges from desert shrub at lower altitudes, up to grasslands with the evergreen manzanita shrub and shrub live oak (*Quercus turbinella*) at higher levels.

ALL PHOTOGRAPHS:
Coconino National Forest, Arizona, USA
At Coconino (above), deserts at lower altitudes give way to forests at higher elevations.

The quaking aspen (*Populus tremuloides*) (far left) is the most widely distributed tree in North America, found from Canada to Central Mexico. It is called 'quaking' because the stalk that attaches the leaf to the stem can twist the leaf to face the sun.

Named after its spikey stems, the hedgehog cactus (*Echinocereus engelmannii*) (left) is a low-growing succulent found across the southwestern United States.

OPPOSITE:

Gila National Forest, New Mexico, USA

In 1924 in the Gila National Forest, the first designated wilderness in the USA was established. Resisting a proposal to build a new road, the Forest Service instead set aside these 305,547 hectares (755,000 acres) of land, deciding that it was to be left roadless and preserved for wilderness recreation. The Gila National Forest gives its name to, among other species, the Gila monster lizard, the Gila trout and the Gila woodpecker.

LEFT:

Pisgah National Forest, North Carolina, USA

Established in 1916, Pisgah National Forest was one of the first national forests in the eastern United States. Located in the Appalachian Mountains, Pisgah – which is the Hebrew word for 'mountain summit' – is a hardwood forest with some of the highest peaks east of the Mississippi River.

ALL PHOTOGRAPHS:

**Blue Ridge Mountains,
Virginia, USA**

These mountains look blue
in the haze because the
trees release the compound
isoprene into the atmosphere.
Part of the Appalachians, the
Blue Ridge Mountains stretch
800km (500 miles) from
southern Pennsylvania south
to Georgia. They are mainly
populated with broadleaf
forests of oak and hickory.

Today the Appalachians are
densely covered in trees, but
by 1895, logging for timber
had reduced the range to, in
places, 'stumps and ashes'.
Through publicly-led planting
efforts, coupled with the rural
population decreasing and
so allowing trees to
grow back naturally, the
Appalachians are now heavily
wooded once again.

Native to the Eastern
North America, the flowering
dogwood tree (*Cornus
florida*) (opposite top) is the
state tree and state flower
of Virginia.

Originating in the
Mediterranean region, the
Purple Periwinkle (*Vinca
minor*) (opposite bottom) was
introduced to North America
by Europeans in the 1700s.

White Mountain National Forest, New Hampshire, USA

Part of the northern Appalachians, the White Mountains National Forest was established in 1918 under the Weeks Act, named after Massachusetts' Congressman John W. Weeks. Coming into force in 1911, the act was initially conceived because the federal government owned no large tracts of land for conservation in the eastern United States. Through purchases of private land, the act had, within a century, protected 80,000 sq km (49,700 sq miles) of forestland.

187

OPPOSITE:

Tehuacán-Cuicatlán Biosphere Reserve, Puebla and Oaxaca, Mexico

There are 70 species of columnar cacti in Mexico and 45 of them have been found in the Tehuacán-Cuicatlán Biosphere Reserve. A major site in the development of agriculture in Mesoamerica, the valley has been the focus of study on the domestication of American foods such as avocadoes, pumpkins, beans, chillies and maize.

RIGHT:

Yaxchilan, Chiapas, Mexico

On the banks of the River Usumacinta, the Mayan city of Yaxchilan rose in the 4th century CE, peaked in the 8th century and collapsed in the early 9th century. After that, it was slowly engulfed by the Lacandon Jungle, before being explored again in the 19th century. A lower montane rainforest thick with vines and ferns, the jungle still hides many more unexcavated Mayan ruins.

Central and South America

Whereas humans take their food from other animals and, ultimately, plant species, trees are fed by carbon dioxide in the air, by water from their roots, and by the sun. Forests are 'carbon sinks': they draw in carbon dioxide, such as the volumes produced through burning fossil fuels, and, until the tree begins to rot or is chopped down and burned, hold that carbon. If we chop down more old trees, not only are we reducing the planet's capacity to absorb carbon dioxide, but we are also releasing more carbon: the tree is burned and processed, exposing more land to be heated by the sun, removing the cooling effect that a tree canopy provides and its ability to capture moisture.

As the planet tries to reduce its carbon emissions and protect its forests from legal and illegal logging, as well as the unsustainable exploitation of its trees, can we find some more immediate stories that give us hope? Yes, there are some. Scientists are often surprised by the resilience of forests and wildlife. After the 1960s, El Salvador lost 90 per cent of its forests to, predominantly, sugar and coffee plantations, but of its 500 bird species, only three disappeared. Then, the upheaval of the civil war in the 1980s left farmland abandoned. And, with no replanting, no initiative from governments or conservationists, native tree species began to reclaim the land.

OPPOSITE:
El Yunque National Forest, Puerto Rico
Puerto Rico is an unincorporated US territory, making El Yunque the only tropical rainforest in the United States National Forest system. Different altitudes in El Yunque feature different forest types. Pictured is the Sierra Palm Tree Forest which is dominated by the Sierran palm (*Prestoea montana*).

ALL PHOTOGRAPHS:

Monteverde Cloud Forest Reserve, Puntarenas and Alajuela, Costa Rica

The Monteverde Cloud Forest Reserve covers more than 10,500 hectares (26,000 acres) of land, 90 per cent of which is primeval cloud forest. Cloud forests are evergreen forests characterised by frequent or seasonal low-level cloud cover.

Monteverde is home to 50 hummingbird species (opposite) and 500 species of orchids, including the spotted ponthieva orchid (*Ponthieva maculata*) (far left).

Hummingbirds, bats and butterflies feed on jungle cucumbers (*Gurania makoyana*) (left), a New World tropical vine.

Monteverde Cloud Forest Reserve, Puntarenas and Alajuela, Costa Rica

What links this cloud forest, the Korean War and Quakers from the United States? In the early 1950s, a group of conscientious objectors, led by Quakers from Alabama, bought land in Costa Rica to avoid being drafted for service in the Korean War. They named the area they settled in Monteverde and worked in dairy and cheese production. Twenty years later, they began efforts to protect the land from further development and established the cloud forest reserve.

The Arenal volcano (right) was dormant for hundreds of years before erupting in 1968 and destroying a small town. Further occasional eruptions happened over the next 40 years, but since 2010 the volcano has been dormant.

Tree cover in Costa Rica declined from 75 per cent in 1940 to 20 per cent in the late 1980s. Much of the land was deforested for logging and cattle farming. In the early 1990s, financial incentives were given to farmers to replant forests or allow them to grow back naturally. Managed ecotourism replaced some of the income from cattle farming. By 2021, more than half of the country was once again covered in forested land. In Monteverde, more than 70,000 tourists visit each year.

ALL PHOTOGRAHS:

Montecristo National Park, El Salvador

War can have many casualties – including farmland. The civil war in El Salvador during the 1980s left whole areas abandoned by farmers. But in time, the farmland was reclaimed by the forests. Since the conflict, there has been an increase of about 40 per cent of forested land across the country.

Located in the far northwest of El Salvador, the Montecristo National Park was established in 2008. With parks in neighbouring Guatemala and Honduras, it forms the Trifinio Fraternidad Transboundary Biosphere Reserve. Montecristo's cloud forest is dominated by oak and laurel trees.

ALL PHOTOGRAPHS:

Río Plátano Biosphere Reserve, La Mosquitia, Honduras
Sloping down to the Caribbean coast, this reserve includes both mountainous and lowland tropical rainforest. Broadleaf gallery forests grow along the major rivers. The reserve's rare or endangered mammals include the West Indian manatee (*Trichechus manatus*), the jaguar (*Panthera onca*) and the giant anteater (*Myrmecophaga tridactyla*).

Despite its protected status, the reserve doesn't have the funds to employ guards and it is the target of illegal logging of mahogany and other trees. Also, more than 2,000 indigenous people live within the reserve and, as their population grows, they seek more forest land to clear for farming.

ALL PHOTOGRAPHS:

La Tigra National Park, Francisco Morazán Department, Honduras
In the highland heart of Honduras, La Tigra National Park has more than 238 sq km (92 sq miles) of cloud forest. Its lowest elevation is 1,800m (5,900ft) and its highest 2,185m (7,170ft). The main tree species are types of pines, as well as the cockspur coral tree (*Erythrina crista-galli*) and oaks, including the evergreen southern live oak (*Quercus virginiana*).

Mammals include pumas, ocelots and white-tailed deer. Among the bird species, there are quetzals, toucans and hummingbirds, such as the green-breasted mountaingem (*Lampornis sybillae*) hummingbird (left), which is only found in Honduras and some parts of Nicaragua.

ALL PHOTOGRAPHS:

Bellavista Cloud Forest Reserve, Pichincha Province, Ecuador

On the northwestern slopes of the Andes Mountains, the Bellavista Cloud Forest Reserve was established by a British-Colombian couple in 1991. Located at more than 2,000m (6,562ft) above sea level, the forest is cool and humid.

Psammisia aberrans (right) is a climbing flowering plant found in Ecuador, Colombia and Peru. It is pollinated by hummingbirds, of which a great variety, from the white-booted racket-tail (*Ocreatus underwoodii*) to the purple-bibbed whitetip (*Urosticte benjamini*), can be seen at Bellavista.

Tree ferns (from the family Cyatheaceae) (far right) have some of the longest fronds in the plant kingdom with some extending up to 4m (13ft). Ferns are found worldwide, but their greatest diversity is in tropical rainforests.

ALL PHOTOGRAPHS:
Central Suriname Nature Reserve, Sipaliwini District, Suriname
The granite dome of Voltzberg Mountain (left) rises above the tropical rainforest of the Central Suriname Nature Reserve. More than 5,000 different plant species have been collected in the reserve's montane and lowland forests. There are also areas of swamp forest.

Squirrel monkeys (far left) from the genus *Saimiri* are found in tropical forests across Central and South America. They mainly eat fruit and insects. They only have sweat glands in the palms of their hands and soles of their feet. Other than seeking out shaded areas to shelter from the sun, they cool themselves by rubbing their bodies in their own urine.

ALL PHOTOGRAPHS:

Quindío wax palms, Cocora Valley, Quindío, Colombia
Around the Christian world on the Sunday before Easter, churches hand out palms to their congregations, commemorating the day when Jesus's followers honoured his final entry into Jerusalem by laying palms in his path. But in Colombia, this practice, along with habitat loss and disease, led to Quindío palms (*Ceroxylon quindiuense*) becoming a threatened species as too many people tore palms off young trees. In 1985, the country gave the Quindío – its national tree – protected status. It is the tallest palm in the world, usually reaching up to 45m (148ft), and only grows in the montane forests of Colombia and Peru.

Noel Kempff Mercado National Park, Province of José Miguel de Velasco, Bolivia

With a vast altitudinal range from 200m (656ft) to nearly 1,000m (3,281ft), this park features a huge variety of habitat types, from swamps and savannahs to evergreen rainforests, palm forests, gallery forests (those that develop alongside rivers in landscapes that otherwise have few or no trees), and dry, deciduous forests.

Originally known as the Parque Nacional Huanchaca, the park was renamed in 1988 when Bolivian conservationist Noel Kempff Mercado and his team were murdered after stumbling across drug traffickers in the park.

Poached for its pelt, the giant otter (*Pteronura brasiliensis*) (below) is now an endangered species. It mainly eats fish and its only predator is humans, though it does compete fiercely with other otters, jaguars and crocodiles for food.

ALL PHOTOGRAPHS:

Manu National Park, Madre de Dios and Cusco, Peru
Located where the Tropical Andes and the Amazonian lowland meet, the Manu National Park has great biodiversity, including more than 4,000 plant species, more than 100 tree species and 800 species of birds.

The fruit of a cocoa tree (*Theobroma cacao*) (left) contains the seeds used to make chocolate. A native species from Mexico down to the Amazon, the cocoa tree was domesticated thousands of years ago and cocoa-based drinks were popular in Mesoamerica when Europeans first encountered the Aztecs in Mexico in the early 16th century. The Aztecs also used cocoa beans as a currency.

The red-and-green macaw (*Ara chloropterus*) (right) is widespread across the forests of northern and central South America, though it is critically endangered in Argentina due to habitat disruption, as well as being hunted for meat and for the pet trade.

ALL PHOTOGRAPHS:

Amazon Rainforest

Encompassing 5.5 million sq km (2.1 mllion sq miles), the Amazon rainforest contains an estimated 390 billion trees from 16,000 species. In surface area, it accounts for half of the world's remaining rainforests. It ranges over nine countries: Brazil, Peru, Colombia, Bolivia, Ecuador, French Guiana, Guyana, Surinam and Venezuela.

More than 30 million people across 350 different ethnic groups live in the Amazon. Despite its immense length, there is not a single bridge across the Amazon River. This is not because it is technically impossible but because there are very few roads alongside the river to create sufficient demand. Ferries are used instead.

ALL PHOTOGRAPHS:

Amazon Rainforest
A study published in 2020 revealed that a teaspoon of soil from the Amazon rainforest contained 400 species of fungi (left). The humidity and heat of the rainforest is perfect for fungi, which break down plant matter into the basic elements of carbon, nitrogen, hydrogen and oxygen.

This juvenile Amazon tree boa (*Corallus hortulanus*) (opposite top left) is a non-venomous, medium-sized constrictor that grows to 1.5–2m (5–6.5ft) in length.

The Surinam horned frog, also known as the Amazonian horned frog (*Ceratophrys cornuta*) (opposite left bottom), feeds on other frogs, as well as fish, lizards and mice.

The red-handed howler monkey (*Alouatta belzebul*) (opposite right) is classed as a vulnerable species. Only found in the Amazon rainforest and Brazilian parts of the Atlantic Forest, the monkey is hunted for meat and to be kept as a pet. Logging and new roads have also reduced its habitat.

RIGHT TOP:

Amazon Deforestation, Brazil

A felled hardwood tree. Between January and August 2019, almost a million hectares (2.5 million acres) of rainforest in Brazil was lost – an area the size of Lebanon. Without the trees – and a tree in the Amazon can release 500l (880 pints) of water a day – the air temperature in parts of the forest has risen by around five degrees Celsius (nine degrees Fahrenheit).

RIGHT BOTTOM:

Para State, Brazil

Land has been cleared to grow soya, which is used in animal feed all around the world, from pigs in China to chickens in Britain, as well as in soya sauce and tofu. Native to East Asia, Soya was introduced to South America in the late 19th century. In 2020, Brazil was its largest producer.

FAR RIGHT:

Amazon Rainforest, Peru

In the Peruvian Amazon in the early 17th century, Franciscan missionaries adopted a local Native American fever remedy made from the bark of a tree found in the cloud forests. The bark contained quinine, and for the next 200 years it remained the only known cure around the world for malaria.

ALL PHOTOGRAPHS:

Atlantic Forest, Brazil
The Atlantic Forest reaches from Brazil's Atlantic coast down to Argentina, stretching inland to Paraguay. By the early 1990s, almost 88 per cent of the forest had been lost and converted to farmland for growing coffee and grazing cattle, as well as eucalyptus plantations (for paper production) and housing. However, since 1996, efforts have been made to restore some of the old forest and, simply by being left alone, 2.7 million hectares (6.7 million acres) have regenerated naturally.

The Brazilian tanager (*Ramphocelus bresilius*) (left top) is endemic to eastern Brazil.

The Atlantic Forest treefrog (*Bokermannohyla hylax*) (left bottom) is native to the Brazilian part of the Atlantic Forest.

The Atlantic Forest (right) hosts a number of different eco-regions, from coastal forests and dry forests to mangroves.

ALL PHOTOGRAPHS:

Iguazú National Park, Misiones, Argentina

Yacare caiman (*Caiman yacare*) (right) are found from southern Brazil down to northern Argentina. During the 1980s they were hunted for their skin (to be used in leather goods) and their numbers fell drastically. For a time, they were listed on the IUCN endangered list and Brazil banned the hunting of yacare. Since the mid-1990s, their population has recovered.

The Iguazú National Park (opposite) was created in 1934 to protect the subtropical rainforest around Iguazú Falls. The rainforest is home to more than 2,000 species of plants.

Iguazú Falls, Argentina-Brazil
Three kilometres (1.9 miles) in width, the Iguazú River drops 80m (262ft) at Iguazú Falls. The river forms the border between Argentina and Brazil, before joining the Parana River downstream. The clouds of spray from the falls permanently soak many of the islands in the river, creating humid microclimates that support lush, subtropical vegetation.

Picture Credits